D1042613

Books by Raymond Carver

FICTION

Will You Please Be Quiet, Please?

What We Talk About When We Talk About Love

Cathedral

POETRY

Near Klamath

Winter Insomnia

At Night the Salmon Move

Where Water Comes Together With Other Water

PROSE AND POETRY

Fires

WHERE WATER COMES TOGETHER WITH OTHER WATER

WHERE WATER COMES TOGETHER WITH OTHER WATER

Poems by
RAYMOND CARVER

VINTAGE BOOKS
A Division of Random House
New York

First Vintage Books Edition, April 1986

Copyright © 1984, 1985 by Raymond Carver

All rights reserved under International and Pan-American Copyright Conventions. Published in the United States by Random House, Inc., New York, and simultaneously in Canada by Random House of Canada Limited, Toronto. Originally published by Random House, Inc., in 1985.

Portions of this work first appeared in the following publications: *Crazyhorse, Grand Street, New Letters, The New York Times Magazine, The Ohio Review, The Paris Review, Pequod, Tendril,* and in limited editions from William B. Ewert, Publisher.

"Happiness," "Money," "Grief," "My Crow," and "For Tess" were first published in *Poetry.*

Library of Congress Cataloging-in-Publication Data

Carver, Raymond.
  Where water comes together with other water.

  Originally published: New York: Random House, 1985.
  I. Title.
[PS3553.A7894W44   1986]   813'.54   85-40679
ISBN 0-394-74327-X

Manufactured in the United States of America

for Tess Gallagher
and Morris R. Bond

CONTENTS

THREE

FOUR

FIVE

ONE

WOOLWORTH'S, 1954

Where this floated up from, or why,
I don't know. But thinking about this
since just after Robert called
telling me he'd be here in a few
minutes to go clamming.

How on my first job I worked
under a man named Sol.
Fifty-some years old, but
a stockboy like I was.
Had worked his way
up to nothing. But grateful
for his job, same as me.
He knew everything there was
to know about that dime-store
merchandise and was willing
to show me. I was sixteen, working
for six bits an hour. Loving it
that I was. Sol taught me
what he knew. He was patient,
though it helped I learned fast.

Most important memory
of that whole time: opening
the cartons of women's lingerie.
Underpants, and soft, clingy things
like that. Taking it out
of cartons by the handful. Something
sweet and mysterious about those
things even then. Sol called it
"linger-ey." "Linger-ey?"

What did I know? I called it
that for a while, too. "Linger-ey."

Then I got older. Quit being
a stockboy. Started pronouncing
that frog word right.
I knew what I was talking about!
Went to taking girls out
in hopes of touching that softness,
slipping down those underpants.
And sometimes it happened. God,
they let me. And they *were*
linger-ey, those underpants.
They tended to linger a little
sometimes, as they slipped down
off the belly, clinging lightly
to the hot white skin.
Passing over the hips and buttocks
and beautiful thighs, traveling
faster now as they crossed the knees,
the calves! Reaching the ankles,
brought together for this
occasion. And kicked free
onto the floor of the car and
forgotten about. Until you had
to look for them.

"Linger-ey."

Those sweet girls!
"Linger a little, for thou art fair."
I know who said that. It fits,
and I'll use it. Robert and his
kids and I out there on the flats
with our buckets and shovels.

His kids, who won't eat clams, cutting
up the whole time, saying "Yuck"
or "Ugh" as clams turned
up in the shovels full of sand
and were tossed into the bucket.
Me thinking all the while
of those early days in Yakima.
And smooth-as-silk underpants.
The lingering kind that Jeanne wore,
and Rita, Muriel, Sue, and her sister,
Cora Mae. All those girls.
Grownup now. Or worse.
I'll say it: dead.

RADIO WAVES

for Antonio Machado

   This rain has stopped, and the moon has come out.
I don't understand the first thing about radio
waves. But I think they travel better just after
a rain, when the air is damp. Anyway, I can reach out
now and pick up Ottawa, if I want to, or Toronto.
Lately, at night, I've found myself
becoming slightly interested in Canadian politics
and domestic affairs. It's true. But mostly it was their
music stations I was after. I could sit here in the chair
and listen, without having to do anything, or think.
I don't have a TV, and I'd quit reading
the papers. At night I turned on the radio.

   When I came out here I was trying to get away
from everything. Especially literature.
What that entails, and what comes after.
There is in the soul a desire for not thinking.
For being still. Coupled with this
a desire to be strict, yes, and rigorous.
But the soul is also a smooth son of a bitch,
not always trustworthy. And I forgot that.
I listened when it said, Better to sing that which is gone
and will not return than that which is still
with us and will be with us tomorrow. Or not.
And if not, that's all right too.
It didn't much matter, it said, if a man sang at all.
That's the voice I listened to.
Can you imagine somebody thinking like this?
That it's really all one and the same?
What nonsense!

But I'd think these stupid thoughts at night
as I sat in the chair and listened to my radio.

Then, Machado, your poetry!
It was a little like a middle-aged man falling
in love again. A remarkable thing to witness,
and embarrassing, too.
Silly things like putting your picture up.
And I took your book to bed with me
and slept with it near at hand. A train went by
in my dreams one night and woke me up.
And the first thing I thought, heart racing
there in the dark bedroom, was this—
It's all right, Machado is here.
Then I could fall back to sleep again.

Today I took your book with me when I went
for my walk. "Pay attention!" you said,
when anyone asked what to do with their lives.
So I looked around and made note of everything.
Then sat down with it in the sun, in my place
beside the river where I could see the mountains.
And I closed my eyes and listened to the sound
of the water. Then I opened them and began to read
"Abel Martin's Last Lamentations."
This morning I thought about you hard, Machado.
And I hope, even in the face of what I know about death,
that you got the message I intended.
But it's okay even if you didn't. Sleep well. Rest.
Sooner or later I hope we'll meet.
And then I can tell you these things myself.

MOVEMENT

Driving lickety-split to make the ferry!
Snow Creek and then Dog Creek
fly by in the headlights.
But the hour's all wrong—no time to think
about the sea-run trout there.
In the lee of the mountains
something on the radio about an old woman
who travels around inside a kettle.
Indigence is at the root of our lives, yes,
but this is not right.
Cut that old woman some slack,
for God's sake.
She's somebody's mother.
You there! It's late. Imagine yourself
with the lid coming down.
The hymns and requiems. The sense of movement
as you're borne along to the next place.

HOMINY AND RAIN

In a little patch of ground beside
the wall of the Earth Sciences building,
a man in a canvas hat was on
his knees doing something in the rain
with some plants. Piano music
came from an upstairs window
in the building next door. Then
the music stopped.
And the window was brought down.

You told me those white blossoms
on the cherry trees in the Quad
smelled like a can of just-opened
hominy. Hominy. They reminded you
of that. This may or may not
be true. I can't say.
I've lost my sense of smell,
along with any interest I may ever
have expressed in working
on my knees with plants, or
vegetables. There was a barefoot

madman with a ring in his ear
playing his guitar and singing
reggae. I remember that.
Rain puddling around his feet.
The place he'd picked to stand
had Welcome Fear
painted on the sidewalk in red letters.

At the time it seemed important
to recall the man on his knees

in front of his plants.
The blossoms. Music of one kind,
and another. Now I'm not so sure.
I can't say, for sure.

It's a little like some tiny cave-in,
in my brain. There's a sense
that I've lost—not everything,
not everything, but far too much.
A part of my life forever.
Like hominy.

Even though your arm stayed linked
in mine. Even though that. Even
though we stood quietly in the
doorway as the rain picked up.
And watched it without saying
anything. Stood quietly.
At peace, I think. Stood watching
the rain. While the one
with the guitar played on.

THE ROAD

What a rough night! It's either no dreams at all,
or else a dream that may or may not be
a dream portending loss. Last night I was dropped off
without a word on a country road.
A house back in the hills showed a light
no bigger than a star.
But I was afraid to go there, and kept walking.

Then to wake up to rain striking the glass.
Flowers in a vase near the window.
The smell of coffee, and you touching your hair
with a gesture like someone who has been gone for years.
But there's a piece of bread under the table
near your feet. And a line of ants
moving back and forth from a crack in the floor.
You've stopped smiling.

Do me a favor this morning. Draw the curtain and come
    back to bed.
Forget the coffee. We'll pretend
we're in a foreign country, and in love.

FEAR

Fear of seeing a police car pull into the drive.
Fear of falling asleep at night.
Fear of not falling asleep.
Fear of the past rising up.
Fear of the present taking flight.
Fear of the telephone that rings in the dead of night.
Fear of electrical storms.
Fear of the cleaning woman who has a spot on her cheek!
Fear of dogs I've been told won't bite.
Fear of anxiety!
Fear of having to identify the body of a dead friend.
Fear of running out of money.
Fear of having too much, though people will not believe this.
Fear of psychological profiles.
Fear of being late and fear of arriving before anyone else.
Fear of my children's handwriting on envelopes.
Fear they'll die before I do, and I'll feel guilty.
Fear of having to live with my mother in her old age, and mine.
Fear of confusion.
Fear this day will end on an unhappy note.
Fear of waking up to find you gone.
Fear of not loving and fear of not loving enough.
Fear that what I love will prove lethal to those I love.
Fear of death.
Fear of living too long.
Fear of death.
      I've said that.

ROMANTICISM

*(for Linda Gregg,
after reading "Classicism")*

The nights are very unclear here.
But if the moon is full, we know it.
We feel one thing one minute,
something else the next.

THE ASHTRAY

*You could write a story about this
ashtray, for example, and a man and a
woman. But the man and woman are
always the two poles of your story.
The North Pole and the South. Every
story has these two poles—he and she.*
A. P. Chekov

They're alone at the kitchen table in her friend's
apartment. They'll be alone for another hour, and then
her friend will be back. Outside, it's raining—
the rain coming down like needles, melting last week's
snow. They're smoking and using the ashtray . . . Maybe
just one of them is smoking . . . *He's* smoking! Never
mind. Anyway, the ashtray is filling up with
cigarettes and ashes.

She's ready to break into tears at any minute.
To plead with him, in fact, though she's proud
and has never asked for anything in her life.
He sees what's coming, recognizes the signs—
a catch in her voice as she brings her fingers
to her locket, the one her mother left her.
He pushes back his chair, gets up, goes over to
the window . . . He wishes it were tomorrow and he
were at the races. He wishes he was out walking,
using his umbrella . . . He strokes his mustache
and wishes he were anywhere except here. But
he doesn't have any choice in the matter. He's got
to put a good face on this for everybody's sake.
God knows, he never meant for things to come
to this. But it's sink or swim now. A wrong
move and he stands to lose her friend, too.

Her breathing slows. She watches him but
doesn't say anything. She knows, or thinks she
knows, where this is leading. She passes a hand
over her eyes, leans forward and puts her head
in her hands. She's done this a few times
before, but has no idea it's something
that drives him wild. He looks away and grinds
his teeth. He lights a cigarette, shakes out
the match, stands a minute longer at the window.

Then walks back to the table and sits
down with a sigh. He drops the match in the ashtray.
She reaches for his hand, and he lets her
take it. Why not? Where's the harm?
Let her. His mind's made up. She covers his
fingers with kisses, tears fall onto his wrist.

He draws on his cigarette and looks at her
as a man would look indifferently on
a cloud, a tree, or a field of oats at sunset.
He narrows his eyes against the smoke. From time
to time he uses the ashtray as he waits
for her to finish weeping.

STILL LOOKING OUT FOR NUMBER ONE

Now that you've gone away for five days,
I'll smoke all the cigarettes I want,
where I want. Make biscuits and eat them
with jam and fat bacon. Loaf. Indulge
myself. Walk on the beach if I feel
like it. And I feel like it, alone and
thinking about when I was young. The people
then who loved me beyond reason.
And how I loved them above all others.
Except one. I'm saying I'll do everything
I want here while you're away!
But there's one thing I won't do.
I won't sleep in our bed without you.
No. It doesn't please me to do so.
I'll sleep where I damn well feel like it—
where I sleep best when you're away
and I can't hold you the way I do.
On the broken sofa in my study.

WHERE WATER COMES TOGETHER WITH OTHER WATER

I love creeks and the music they make.
And rills, in glades and meadows, before
they have a chance to become creeks.
I may even love them best of all
for their secrecy. I almost forgot
to say something about the source!
Can anything be more wonderful than a spring?
But the big streams have my heart too.
And the places streams flow into rivers.
The open mouths of rivers where they join the sea.
The places where water comes together
with other water. Those places stand out
in my mind like holy places.
But these coastal rivers!
I love them the way some men love horses
or glamorous women. I have a thing
for this cold swift water.
Just looking at it makes my blood run
and my skin tingle. I could sit
and watch these rivers for hours.
Not one of them like any other.
I'm 45 years old today.
Would anyone believe it if I said
I was once 35?
My heart empty and sere at 35!
Five more years had to pass
before it began to flow again.
I'll take all the time I please this afternoon
before leaving my place alongside this river.
It pleases me, loving rivers.

Loving them all the way back
to their source.
Loving everything that increases me.

TWO

HAPPINESS

So early it's still almost dark out.
I'm near the window with coffee,
and the usual early morning stuff
that passes for thought.
When I see the boy and his friend
walking up the road
to deliver the newspaper.
They wear caps and sweaters,
and one boy has a bag over his shoulder.
They are so happy
they aren't saying anything, these boys.
I think if they could, they would take
each other's arm.
It's early in the morning,
and they are doing this thing together.
They come on, slowly.
The sky is taking on light,
though the moon still hangs pale over the water.
Such beauty that for a minute
death and ambition, even love,
doesn't enter into this.
Happiness. It comes on
unexpectedly. And goes beyond, really,
any early morning talk about it.

THE OLD DAYS

You'd dozed in front of the TV
but you hadn't been to bed yet
when you called. I was asleep,
or nearly, when the phone rang.
You wanted to tell me you'd thrown
a party. And I was missed.
It was like the old days, you
said, and laughed.
Dinner was a disaster.
Everybody dead drunk by the time
food hit the table. People
were having a good time, a great
time, a hell of a time, until
somebody took somebody
else's fiancée upstairs. Then
somebody pulled a knife.

But you got in front of the guy
as he was going upstairs
and talked him down.
Disaster narrowly averted,
you said, and laughed again.
You didn't remember much else
of what happened after that.
People got into their coats
and began to leave. You
must have dropped off for a few
minutes in front of the TV
because it was screaming at you
to get it a drink when you woke up.
Anyway, you're in Pittsburgh,
and I'm in here in this

little town on the other side
of the country. Most everyone
has cleared out of our lives now.
You wanted to call me up and say hello.
To say you were thinking
about me, and of the old days.
To say you were missing me.

It was then I remembered
back to those days and how
telephones used to jump when they rang.
And the people who would come
in those early-morning hours
to pound on the door in alarm.
Never mind the alarm felt inside.
I remembered that, and gravy dinners.
Knives lying around, waiting
for trouble. Going to bed
and hoping I wouldn't wake up.

I love you, Bro, you said.
And then a sob passed
between us. I took hold
of the receiver as if
it were my buddy's arm.
And I wished for us both
I could put my arms
around you, old friend.
I love you too, Bro.
I said that, and then we hung up.

OUR FIRST HOUSE
IN SACRAMENTO

This much is clear to me now—even then
our days were numbered. After our first week
in the house that came furnished
with somebody else's things, a man appeared
one night with a baseball bat. And raised it.
I was not the man he thought I was.
Finally, I got him to believe it.
He wept from frustration after his anger
left him. None of this had anything to do
with Beatlemania. The next week these friends
of ours from the bar where we all drank
brought friends of theirs to our house—
and we played poker. I lost the grocery money
to a stranger. Who went on to quarrel
with his wife. In his frustration
he drove his fist through the kitchen wall.
Then he, too, disappeared from my life forever.
When we left that house where nothing worked
any longer, we left at midnight
with a U-Haul trailer and a lantern.
Who knows what passed through the neighbors' minds
when they saw a family leaving their house
in the middle of the night?
The lantern moving behind the curtainless
windows. The shadows going from room to room,
gathering their things into boxes.
I saw firsthand
what frustration can do to a man.
Make him weep, make him throw his fist
through a wall. Set him to dreaming
of the house that's his

at the end of the long road. A house
filled with music, ease, and generosity.
A house that hasn't been lived in yet.

NEXT YEAR

That first week in Santa Barbara wasn't the worst thing
to happen. The second week he fell on his head
while drinking, just before he had to lecture.
In the lounge, that second week, she took the microphone
from the singer's hands and crooned her own
torch song. Then danced. And then passed out
on the table. That's not the worst, either. They
went to jail that second week. He wasn't driving
so they booked him, dressed him in pajamas
and stuck him in Detox. Told him to get some sleep.
Told him he could see about his wife in the morning.
But how could he sleep when they wouldn't let him
close the door to his room?
The corridor's green light entered,
and the sound of a man weeping.
His wife had been called upon to give the alphabet
beside the road, in the middle of the night.
This is strange enough. But the cops had her
stand on one leg, close her eyes,
and try to touch her nose with her index finger.
All of which she failed to do.
She went to jail for resisting arrest.
He bailed her out when he got out of Detox.
They drove home in ruins.
This is not the worst. Their daughter had picked that night
to run away from home. She left a note:

"You're both crazy. Give me a break, PLEASE.
Don't come after me."
That's still not the worst. They went on
thinking they were the people they said they were.
Answering to those names.
Making love to the people with those names.
Nights without beginning that had no end.
Talking about a past as if it'd really happened.
Telling themselves that this time next year,
this time next year
things were going to be different.

TO MY DAUGHTER

Everything I see will outlive me.
Anna Akhmatova

It's too late now to put a curse on you—wish you
plain, say, as Yeats did his daughter. And when
we met her in Sligo, selling her paintings, it'd worked—
she *was* the plainest, oldest woman in Ireland.
But she was safe.
For the longest time, his reasoning
escaped me. Anyway, it's too late for you,
as I said. You're grownup now, and lovely.
You're a beautiful drunk, daughter.
But you're a drunk. I can't say you're breaking
my heart. I don't have a heart when it comes
to this booze thing. Sad, yes, Christ alone knows.
Your old man, the one they call Shiloh, is back
in town, and the drink has started to flow again.
You've been drunk for three days, you tell me,
when you know goddamn well drinking is like poison
to our family. Didn't your mother and I set you
example enough? Two people
who loved each other knocking each other around,
knocking back the love we felt, glass by empty glass,
curses and blows and betrayals?
You must be crazy! Wasn't all that enough for you?
You want to die? Maybe that's it. Maybe
I think I know you, and I don't.
I'm not kidding, kiddo. Who are you kidding?
Daughter, you can't drink.
The last few times I saw you, you were out of it.
A cast on your collarbone, or else
a splint on your finger, dark glasses to hide
your beautiful bruised eyes. A lip

that a man should kiss instead of split.
Oh, Jesus, Jesus, Jesus Christ!
You've got to take hold now.
Do you hear me? Wake up! You've got to knock it off
and get straight. Clean up your act. I'm asking you.
Okay, telling you. Sure, our family was made
to squander, not collect. But turn this around now.
You simply must—that's all!
Daughter, you can't drink.
It will kill you. Like it did your mother, and me.
Like it did.

ANATHEMA

The entire household suffered.
My wife, myself, the two children, and the dog
whose puppies were born dead.
Our affairs, such as they were, withered.
My wife was dropped by her lover,
the one-armed teacher of music who was
her only contact with the outside world
and the things of the mind.
My own girlfriend said she couldn't stand it
anymore, and went back to her husband.
The water was shut off.
All that summer the house baked.
The peach trees were blasted.
Our little flower bed lay trampled.
The brakes went out on the car, and the battery
failed. The neighbors quit speaking
to us and closed their doors in our faces.
Checks flew back at us from merchants—
and then mail stopped being delivered
altogether. Only the sheriff got through
from time to time—with one or the other
of our children in the back seat,
pleading to be taken anywhere but here.
And then mice entered the house in droves.
Followed by a bull snake. My wife
found it sunning itself in the living room
next to the dead TV. How she dealt with it
is another matter. Chopped its head off
right there on the floor.
And then chopped it in two when it continued
to writhe. We saw we couldn't hold out
any longer. We were beaten.

We wanted to get down on our knees
and say forgive us our sins, forgive us
our lives. But it was too late.
Too late. No one around would listen.
We had to watch as the house was pulled down,
the ground plowed up, and then
we were dispersed in four directions.

ENERGY

Last night at my daughter's, near Blaine,
she did her best to tell me
what went wrong
between her mother and me.
"Energy. You two's energy was all wrong."
She looks like her mother
when her mother was young.
Laughs like her.
Moves the drift of hair
from her forehead, like her mother.
Can take a cigarette down
to the filter in three draws,
just like her mother. I thought
this visit would be easy. Wrong.
This is hard, brother. Those years
spilling over into my sleep when I try
to sleep. To wake to find a thousand
cigarettes in the ashtray and every
light in the house burning. I can't
pretend to understand anything:
today I'll be carried
three thousand miles away into
the loving arms of another woman, not
her mother. No. She's caught
in the flywheel of a new love.
I turn off the last light
and close the door.
Moving toward whatever ancient thing
it is that works the chains
and pulls us so relentlessly on.

LOCKING YOURSELF OUT,
THEN TRYING TO GET BACK IN

You simply go out and shut the door
without thinking. And when you look back
at what you've done
it's too late. If this sounds
like the story of a life, okay.

It was raining. The neighbors who had
a key were away. I tried and tried
the lower windows. Stared
inside at the sofa, plants, the table
and chairs, the stereo set-up.
My coffee cup and ashtray waited for me
on the glass-topped table, and my heart
went out to them. I said, *Hello, friends,*
or something like that. After all,
this wasn't so bad.
Worse things had happened. This
was even a little funny. I found the ladder.
Took that and leaned it against the house.
Then climbed in the rain to the deck,
swung myself over the railing
and tried the door. Which was locked,
of course. But I looked in just the same
at my desk, some papers, and my chair.
This was the window on the other side
of the desk where I'd raise my eyes
and stare out when I sat at that desk.
This is not like downstairs, I thought.
This is something else.

And it was something to look in like that, unseen,
from the deck. To be there, inside, and not be there.
I don't even think I can talk about it.
I brought my face close to the glass
and imagined myself inside,
sitting at the desk. Looking up
from my work now and again.
Thinking about some other place
and some other time.
The people I had loved then.

I stood there for a minute in the rain.
Considering myself to be the luckiest of men.
Even though a wave of grief passed through me.
Even though I felt violently ashamed
of the injury I'd done back then.
I bashed that beautiful window.
And stepped back in.

MEDICINE

All I know about medicine I picked up
from my doctor friend in El Paso
who drank and took drugs. We were buddies
until I moved East. I'm saying
I was never sick a day in my life.
But something has appeared
on my shoulder and continues to grow.
A wen, I think, and love the word
but not the thing itself, whatever
it is. Late at night my teeth ache
and the phone rings. I'm ill,
unhappy and alone. Lord!
Give me your unsteady knife,
doc. Give me your hand, friend.

WENAS RIDGE

The seasons turning. Memory flaring.
Three of us that fall. Young hoodlums—
shoplifters, stealers of hubcaps.
Bozos. Dick Miller, dead now.
Lyle Rousseau, son of the Ford dealer.
And I, who'd just made a girl pregnant.
Hunting late into that golden afternoon
for grouse. Following deer paths,
pushing through undergrowth, stepping over
blow-downs. Reaching out for something to hold onto.

At the top of Wenas Ridge
we walked out of pine trees and could see
down deep ravines, where the wind roared, to the river.
More alive then, I thought, than I'd ever be.
But my whole life, in switchbacks, ahead of me.

Hawks, deer, coons we looked at and let go.
Killed six grouse and should have stopped.
Didn't, though we had limits.

Lyle and I climbing fifty feet or so
above Dick Miller. Who screamed—"Yaaaah!"
Then swore and swore. Legs numbing as I saw what.
That fat, dark snake rising up. Beginning to sing.
And how it sang! A timber rattler thick as my wrist.
It'd struck at Miller, but missed. No other way
to say it—he was paralyzed. Could scream, and swear,
not shoot. Then the snake lowered itself from sight
and went in under rocks. We understood
we'd have to get down. In the same way we'd got up.
Blindly crawling through brush, stepping over blow-downs,

pushing into undergrowth. Shadows falling from trees now
onto flat rocks that held the day's heat. And snakes.
My heart stopped, and then started again.
My hair stood on end. This was the moment
my life had prepared me for. And I wasn't ready.

We started down anyway. Jesus, please help me
out of this, I prayed. I'll believe in you again
and honor you always. But Jesus was crowded out
of my head by the vision of that rearing snake.
That singing. Keep believing in me, snake said,
for I will return. I made an obscure, criminal pact
that day. Praying to Jesus in one breath.
To snake in the other. Snake finally more real
to me. The memory of that day
like a blow to the calf now.

I got out, didn't I? But something happened.
I married the girl I loved, yet poisoned her life.
Lies began to coil in my heart and call it home.
Got used to darkness and its crooked ways.
Since then I've always feared rattlesnakes.
Been ambivalent about Jesus.
But someone, something's responsible for this.
Now, as then.

READING

Every man's life is a mystery, even as
yours is, and mine. Imagine
a château with a window opening
onto Lake Geneva. There in the window
on warm and sunny days is a man
so engrossed in reading he doesn't look
up. Or if he does he marks his place
with a finger, raises his eyes, and peers
across the water to Mont Blanc,
and beyond, to Selah, Washington,
where he is with a girl
and getting drunk *for the first time*.
The last thing he remembers, before
he passes out, is that she spit on him.
He keeps on drinking
and getting spit on for years.
But some people will tell you
that suffering is good for the character.
You're free to believe anything.
In any case, he goes
back to reading and will not
feel guilty about his mother
drifting in her boat of sadness,
or consider his children
and their troubles that go on and on.
Nor does he intend to think about
the clear-eyed woman he once loved
and her defeat at the hands of eastern religion.
Her grief has no beginning, and no end.
Let anyone in the château, or Selah,
come forward who might claim kin with the man
who sits all day in the window reading,

like a picture of a man reading.
Let the sun come forward.
Let the man himself come forward.
What in Hell can he be reading?

RAIN

Woke up this morning with
a terrific urge to lie in bed all day
and read. Fought against it for a minute.

Then looked out the window at the rain.
And gave over. Put myself entirely
in the keep of this rainy morning.

Would I live my life over again?
Make the same unforgivable mistakes?
Yes, given half a chance. Yes.

MONEY

In order to be able to live
on the right side of the law.
To always use his own name
and phone number. To go bail
for a friend and not give
a damn if the friend skips town.
Hope, in fact, she does.
To give some money
to his mother. And to his
children and their mother.
Not save it. He wants
to use it up before it's gone.
Buy clothes with it.
Pay the rent and utilities.
Buy food, and then some.
Go out for dinner when he feels like it.
And it's okay
to order anything off the menu!
Buy drugs when he wants.
Buy a car. If it breaks
down, repair it. Or else
buy another. See that
boat? He might buy one
just like it. And sail it
around the Horn, looking
for company. He knows a girl
in Porto Alegre who'd love
to see him in
his own boat, sails full,
turn into the harbor for her.
A fellow who could afford
to come all this way

to see her. Just because
he liked the sound
of her laughter,
and the way she swings her hair.

ASPENS

Imagine a young man, alone, without anyone.
The moment a few raindrops streaked his glass
he began to scribble.
He lived in a tenement with mice for company.
I loved his bravery.

Someone else a few doors down
played Segovia records all day.
He never left his room, and no one could blame him.
At night he could hear the other's
typewriter going, and feel comforted.

Literature and music.
Everyone dreaming of Spanish horsemen
and courtyards.
Processions. Ceremony, and
resplendence.

Aspen trees.
Days of rain and high water.
Leaves hammered into the ground finally.
In my heart, this plot of earth
that the storm lights.

THREE

AT LEAST

I want to get up early one more morning,
before sunrise. Before the birds, even.
I want to throw cold water on my face
and be at my work table
when the sky lightens and smoke
begins to rise from the chimneys
of the other houses.
I want to see the waves break
on this rocky beach, not just hear them
break as I did all night in my sleep.
I want to see again the ships
that pass through the Strait from every
seafaring country in the world—
old, dirty freighters just barely moving along,
and the swift new cargo vessels
painted every color under the sun
that cut the water as they pass.
I want to keep an eye out for them.
And for the little boat that plies
the water between the ships
and the pilot station near the lighthouse.
I want to see them take a man off the ship
and put another up on board.
I want to spend the day watching this happen
and reach my own conclusions.
I hate to seem greedy—I have so much
to be thankful for already.
But I want to get up early one more morning, at least.
And go to my place with some coffee and wait.
Just wait, to see what's going to happen.

THE GRANT

It's either this or bobcat hunting
with my friend Morris.
Trying to write a poem at six this
morning, or else running
behind the hounds with
a rifle in my hands.
Heart jumping in its cage.
I'm 45 years old. No occupation.
Imagine the luxuriousness of this life.
Try and imagine.
May go with him if he goes
tomorrow. But may not.

MY BOAT

My boat is being made to order. Right now it's about to leave
the hands of its builders. I've reserved a special place
for it down at the marina. It's going to have plenty of room
on it for all my friends: Richard, Bill, Chuck, Toby, Jim, Hayden,
Gary, George, Harold, Don, Dick, Scott, Geoffrey, Jack,
Paul, Jay, Morris, and Alfredo. All my friends! They know who
    they are.
Tess, of course. I wouldn't go anyplace without her.
And Kristina, Merry, Catherine, Diane, Sally, Annick, Pat,
    Judith, Susie, Lynne, Annie, Jane, Mona.
Doug and Amy! They're family, but they're also my friends,
and they like a good time. There's room on my boat
for just about everyone. I'm serious about this!
There'll be a place on board for everyone's stories.
My own, but also the ones belonging to my friends.
Short stories, and the ones that go on and on. The true
and the made-up. The ones already finished, and the ones still
    being written.
Poems, too! Lyric poems, and the longer, darker narratives.
For my painter friends, paints and canvases will be on board
    my boat.
We'll have fried chicken, lunch meats, cheeses, rolls,
French bread. Every good thing that my friends and I like.
And a big basket of fruit, in case anyone wants fruit.
In case anyone wants to say he or she ate an apple,
or some grapes, on my boat. Whatever my friends want,
name it, and it'll be there. Soda pop of all kinds.
Beer and wine, sure. No one will be denied anything, on
    my boat.
We'll go out into the sunny harbor and have fun, that's the idea.
Just have a good time all around. Not thinking
about this or that or getting ahead or falling behind.

Fishing poles if anyone wants to fish. The fish are out there!
We may even go a little way down the coast, on my boat.
But nothing dangerous, nothing too serious.
The idea is simply to enjoy ourselves and not get scared.
We'll eat and drink and laugh a lot, on my boat.
I've always wanted to take at least one trip like this,
with my friends, on my boat. If we want to
we'll listen to Schumann on the CBC.
But if that doesn't work out, okay,
we'll switch to KRAB, The Who, and the Rolling Stones.
Whatever makes my friends happy! Maybe everyone
will have their own radio, on my boat. In any case,
we're going to have a big time. People are going to have fun,
and do what they want to do, on my boat.

THE POEM I DIDN'T WRITE

Here is the poem I was going to write
earlier, but didn't
because I heard you stirring.
I was thinking again
about that first morning in Zurich.
How we woke up before sunrise.
Disoriented for a minute. But going
out onto the balcony that looked down
over the river, and the old part of the city.
And simply standing there, speechless.
Nude. Watching the sky lighten.
So thrilled and happy. As if
we'd been put there
just at that moment.

WORK

for John Gardner, d. September 14, 1982

Love of work. The blood singing
in that. The fine high rise
of it into the work. A man says,
I'm working. Or, I worked today.
Or, I'm trying to make it work.
Him working seven days a week.
And being awakened in the morning
by his young wife, his head on the typewriter.
The fullness before work.
The amazed understanding after.
Fastening his helmet.
Climbing onto his motorcycle
and thinking about home.
And work. Yes, work. The going
to what lasts.

IN THE YEAR 2020

Which of us will be left then—
old, dazed, unclear—
but willing to talk about our dead friends?
Talk and talk, like an old faucet leaking.
So that the young ones,
respectful, touchingly curious,
will find themselves stirred
by the recollections.
By the very mention of this name
or that name, and what we did together.
(As we were respectful, but curious
and excited, to hear someone tell
about the illustrious dead ahead of us.)
Of which of us will they say
to their friends,
he knew so and so! He was friends with ————
and they spent time together.
He was at that big party.
Everyone was there. They celebrated
and danced until dawn. They put their arms
around each other and danced
until the sun came up.
Now they're all gone.
Of which of us will it be said—
he knew them? Shook hands with them
and embraced them, stayed overnight
in their warm houses. Loved them!

Friends, I do love you, it's true.
And I hope I'm lucky enough, privileged enough,
to live on and bear witness.
Believe me, I'll say only the most

glorious things about you and our time here!
For the survivor there has to be something
to look forward to. Growing old,
losing everything and everybody.

THE JUGGLER AT *HEAVEN'S GATE*

for Michael Cimino

Behind the dirty table where Kristofferson is having
breakfast, there's a window that looks onto a nineteenth-
century street in Sweetwater, Wyoming. A juggler
is at work out there, wearing a top hat and a frock coat,
a little reed of a fellow keeping three sticks
in the air. Think about this for a minute.
This juggler. This amazing act of the mind and hands.
A man who juggles for a living.
Everyone in his time has known a star,
or a gunfighter. Somebody, anyway, who pushes somebody
around. But a juggler! Blue smoke hangs inside
this awful café, and over that dirty table where two
grownup men talk about a woman's future. And something,
something about the Cattlemen's Association.
But the eye keeps going back to that juggler.
That tiny spectacle. At this minute, Ella's plight
or the fate of the emigrants
is not nearly so important as this juggler's exploits.
How'd *he* get into the act, anyway? What's his story?
That's the story I want to know. Anybody
can wear a gun and swagger around. Or fall in love
with somebody who loves somebody else. But to *juggle*
for God's sake! To give your life to that.
To go with that. Juggling.

MY DAUGHTER AND APPLE PIE

She serves me a piece of it a few minutes
out of the oven. A little steam rises
from the slits on top. Sugar and spice—
cinnamon—burned into the crust.
But she's wearing these dark glasses
in the kitchen at ten o'clock
in the morning—everything nice—
as she watches me break off
a piece, bring it to my mouth,
and blow on it. My daughter's kitchen,
in winter. I fork the pie in
and tell myself to stay out of it.
She says she loves him. No way
could it be worse.

COMMERCE

A swank dinner. Food truly wonderful
and plenty of it. It was the way I always dreamed
it would be. And it just kept coming
while we talked about the bottom line.
Even when we weren't talking about it,
it was there—in the oysters, the lamb,
the sauces, the fine white linen, the cutlery
and goblets. It said, Here is your life, enjoy.
This is the poem I wanted to live to write! Then
to come upon the spirit in a flaming dessert—
the streaks of fire shooting up, only to drop
back, as if exhausted.

Driving home afterwards, my head aswim
from overeating. What a swine! I deserve
everything that fellow's going to say about me.
Falling asleep in my pants on top of the covers.
But not before thinking about wolves,
a sultry day in the woods.
My life staked down in the clearing.
When I try to turn my head to reveal
the fleshy neck, I can't move.
I don't have the energy. Let them go
for the belly, those brother wolves
with the burning eyes.
To have come this far in a single night!
But then I never knew when to stop.

THE FISHING POLE OF
THE DROWNED MAN

I didn't want to use it at first.
Then I thought, no, it would
give up secrets and bring me luck—
that's what I needed then.
Besides, he'd left it behind for me
to use when he went swimming that time.
Shortly afterwards, I met two women.
One of them loved opera and the other
was a drunk who'd done time
in jail. I took up with one
and began to drink and fight a lot.
The way this woman could sing and carry on!
We went straight to the bottom.

A WALK

I took a walk on the railroad track.
Followed that for a while
and got off at the country graveyard
where a man sleeps between
two wives. Emily van der Zee,
Loving Wife and Mother,
is at John van der Zee's right.
Mary, the second Mrs. van der Zee,
also a Loving Wife, to his left.
First Emily went, then Mary.
After a few years, the old fellow himself.
Eleven children came from these unions.
And they, too, would all have to be dead now.
This is a quiet place. As good a place as any
to break my walk, sit, and provide against
my own death, which comes on.
But I don't understand, and I don't understand.
All I know about this fine, sweaty life,
my own or anyone else's,
is that in a little while I'll rise up
and leave this astonishing place
that gives shelter to dead people. This graveyard.
And go. Walking first on one rail
and then the other.

MY DAD'S WALLET

Long before he thought of his own death,
my dad said he wanted to lie close
to his parents. He missed them so
after they went away.
He said this enough that my mother remembered,
and I remembered. But when the breath
left his lungs and all signs of life
had faded, he found himself in a town
512 miles away from where he wanted most to be.

My dad, though. He was restless
even in death. Even in death
he had this one last trip to take.
All his life he liked to wander,
and now he had one more place to get to.

The undertaker said he'd arrange it,
not to worry. Some poor light
from the window fell on the dusty floor
where we waited that afternoon
until the man came out of the back room
and peeled off his rubber gloves.
He carried the smell of formaldehyde with him.
He was a big man, this undertaker said.
Then began to tell us why
he liked living in this small town.
This man who'd just opened my dad's veins.
How much is it going to cost? I said.

He took out his pad and pen and began
to write. First, the preparation charges.
Then he figured the transportation

of the remains at 22 cents a mile.
But this was a round-trip for the undertaker,
don't forget. Plus, say, six meals
and two nights in a motel. He figured
some more. Add a surcharge of
$210 for his time and trouble,
and there you have it.

He thought we might argue.
There was a spot of color on
each of his cheeks as he looked up
from his figures. The same poor light
fell in the same poor place on
the dusty floor. My mother nodded
as if she understood. But she
hadn't understood a word of it.
None of it had made any sense to her,
beginning with the time she left home
with my dad. She only knew
that whatever was happening
was going to take money.
She reached into her purse and brought up
my dad's wallet. The three of us
in that little room that afternoon.
Our breath coming and going.

We stared at the wallet for a minute.
Nobody said anything.
All the life had gone out of that wallet.
It was old and rent and soiled.
But it was my dad's wallet. And she opened
it and looked inside. Drew out
a handful of money that would go
toward this last, most astounding, trip.

FOUR

ASK HIM

Reluctantly, my son goes with me
through the iron gates
of the cemetery in Montparnasse.
"What a way to spend a day in Paris!"
is what he'd like to say. Did, in fact, say.
He speaks French. Has started a conversation
with a white-haired guard who offers himself
as our informal guide. So we move slowly,
the three of us, along row upon row of graves.
Everyone, it seems, is here.

It's quiet, and hot, and the street sounds
of Paris can't reach. The guard wants to steer us
to the grave of the man who invented the submarine,
and Maurice Chevalier's grave. And the grave
of the 28-year-old singer, Nonnie,
covered with a mound of red roses.

I want to see the graves of the writers.
My son sighs. He doesn't want to see any of it.
Has seen enough. He's passed beyond boredom
into resignation. Guy de Maupassant; Sartre; Sainte-Beuve;
Gautier; the Goncourts; Paul Verlaine and his old comrade,
Charles Baudelaire. Where we linger.

None of these names, or graves, have anything to do
with the untroubled lives of my son and the guard.
Who can this morning talk and joke together
in the French language under a fine sun.
But there are several names chiseled on Baudelaire's stone,
and I can't understand why.

Charles Baudelaire's name is between that of his mother,
who loaned him money and worried all her life
about his health, and his stepfather, a martinet
he hated and who hated him and everything he stood for.
"Ask your friend," I say. So my son asks.
It's as if he and the guard are old friends now,
and I'm there to be humored.
The guard says something and then lays
one hand over the other. Like that. Does it
again. One hand over the other. Grinning. Shrugging.
My son translates. But I understand.
"Like a sandwich, Pop," my son says. "A Baudelaire sandwich."

At which the three of us walk on.
The guard would as soon be doing this as something else.
He lights his pipe. Looks at his watch. It's almost time
for his lunch, and a glass of wine.
"Ask him," I say, "if he wants to be buried
in this cemetery when he dies.
Ask him where he wants to be buried."
My son is capable of saying anything.
I recognize the words *tombeau* and *mort*
in his mouth. The guard stops.
It's clear his thoughts have been elsewhere.
Underwater warfare. The music hall, the cinema.
Something to eat and the glass of wine.
Not corruption, no, and the falling away.
Not annihilation. Not his death.

He looks from one to the other of us.
Who are we kidding? Are we making a bad joke?
He salutes and walks away.
Heading for a table at an outdoor café.
Where he can take off his cap, run his fingers
through his hair. Hear laughter and voices.

The heavy clink of silverware. The ringing
of glasses. Sun on the windows.
Sun on the sidewalk and in the leaves.
Sun finding its way onto his table. His glass. His hands.

NEXT DOOR

The woman asked us in for pie. Started
telling about her husband, the man who
used to live there. How he had to be carted
off to the nursing home. He wanted
to cover this fine oak ceiling
with cheap insulation, she said. That was the first
sign of anything being wrong. Then he had
a stroke. A vegetable now. Anyway,
next, the game warden stuck the barrel
of his pistol into her son's ear.
And cocked the hammer. But the kid
wasn't doing that much wrong, and the game
warden is the kid's uncle, don't you see?
So everybody's on the outs. Everybody's
nuts and nobody's speaking to anybody
these days. Here's a big bone the son
found at the mouth of the river.
Maybe it's a human bone? An arm bone
or something? She puts it back on the window-
sill next to a bowl of flowers.
The daughter stays in her room all day,
writing poems about her attempted suicide.
That's why we don't see her. Nobody sees
her anymore. She tears up the poems
and writes them over again. But one of these
days she'll get it right. Would you believe it—
the car threw a rod? That black car
that stands like a hearse
in the yard next door. The engine winched out,
swinging from a tree.

THE CAUCASUS: A ROMANCE

Each evening an eagle soars down from the snowy
crags and passes over camp. It wants to see
if it's true what they say back in Russia: the only
career open to young men these days
is the military. Young men of good family, and a few
others—older, silent men—men who've blotted their
copybooks, as they call it out here. Men like
the Colonel, who lost his ear in a duel.

Dense forests of pine, alder, and birch. Torrents
that fall from dizzying precipices. Mist. Clamorous
rivers. Mountains covered with snow even now, even
in August. Everywhere, as far as the eye can reach,
profusion. A sea of poppies. Wild buckwheat that
shimmers in the heat, that waves and rolls to the horizon.
Panthers. Bees as big as a boy's fist. Bears that won't
get out of a man's way, that will tear a body to
pieces and then go back to the business of rooting
and chuffing like hogs in the rich undergrowth. Clouds
of white butterflies that rise, then settle and
rise again on slopes thick with lilac and fern.

Now and then a real engagement with the enemy.
Much howling from their side, cries, the drum
of horses' hooves, rattle of musket fire, a Chechen's ball
smashing into a man's breast, a stain that blossoms
and spreads, that ripples over the white uniform like crimson
petals opening. Then the chase begins: hearts racing,
minds emptying out entirely as the emperor's young
men, dandies all, gallop over plains, laughing,
yelling their lungs out. Or else they urge
their lathered horses along forest trails, pistols

ready. They burn Chechen crops, kill Chechen stock,
knock down the pitiful villages. They're soldiers,
after all, and these are not maneuvers. Shamil,
the bandit chieftain, he's the one they want most.

At night, a moon broad and deep as a serving dish
sallies out from behind the peaks. But this
moon is only for appearance's sake. Really, it's
armed to the teeth, like everything else out here.
When the Colonel sleeps, he dreams of a drawing room—
one drawing room in particular—oh, clean and elegant,
most comfortable drawing room! Where friends lounge
in plush chairs, or on divans, and drink from
little glasses of tea. In the dream, it is always
Thursday, 2–4. There is a piano next to the window
that looks out on Nevsky Prospect. A young woman
finishes playing, pauses, and turns to the polite
applause. But in the dream it is the Circassian
woman with a saber cut across her face. His friends
draw back in horror. They lower their eyes, bow,
and begin taking their leave. Goodbye, goodbye,
they mutter. In Petersburg they said that out here,
in the Caucasus, sunsets are everything.
But this is not true; sunsets are not enough.
In Petersburg they said the Caucasus is a country that gives
rise to legend, where heroes are born every day.
They said, long ago, in Petersburg, that reputations
were made, and lost, in the Caucasus. *A gravely*
beautiful place, as one of the Colonel's men put it.

The officers serving under him will return
home soon, and more young men will come to take
their places. After the new arrivals dismount
to pay their respects, the Colonel will keep them
waiting a time. Then fix them with a stern but

fatherly gaze, these slim young men with tiny
mustaches and boisterous high spirits, who look
at him and wonder, who ask themselves what it is
he's running from. But he's not running. He likes it
here, in the Caucasus, after a fashion. He's even
grown used to it—or nearly. There's plenty to do,
God knows. Plenty of grim work in the days, and months,
ahead. Shamil is out there in the mountains somewhere—
or maybe he's on the Steppes. The scenery is lovely,
you can be sure, and this but a rough record
of the actual and the passing.

A FORGE, AND A SCYTHE

One minute I had the windows open
and the sun was out. Warm breezes
blew through the room.
(I remarked on this in a letter.)
Then, while I watched, it grew dark.
The water began whitecapping.
All the sport-fishing boats turned
and headed in, a little fleet.
Those wind-chimes on the porch
blew down. The tops of our trees shook.
The stove pipe squeaked and rattled
around in its moorings.
I said, "A forge, and a scythe."
I talk to myself like this.
Saying the names of things—
capstan, hawser, loam, leaf, furnace.
Your face, your mouth, your shoulder
inconceivable to me now!
Where did they go? It's like
I dreamed them. The stones we brought
home from the beach lie face up
on the windowsill, cooling.
Come home. Do you hear?
My lungs are thick with the smoke
of your absence.

THE PIPE

The next poem I write will have firewood
right in the middle of it, firewood so thick
with pitch my friend will leave behind
his gloves and tell me, "Wear these when you
handle that stuff." The next poem
will have night in it, too, and all the stars
in the western hemisphere; and an immense body
of water shining for miles under a new moon.
The next poem will have a bedroom
and living room for itself, skylights,
a sofa, a table and chairs by the window,
a vase of violets cut just an hour before lunch.
There'll be a lamp burning in the next poem;
and a fireplace where pitch-soaked
blocks of fir flame up, consuming one another.
Oh, the next poem will throw sparks!
But there won't be any cigarettes in that poem.
I'll take up smoking the pipe.

LISTENING

It was a night like all the others. Empty
of everything save memory. He thought
he'd got to the other side of things.
But he hadn't. He read a little
and listened to the radio. Looked out the window
for a while. Then went upstairs. In bed
realized he'd left the radio on.
But closed his eyes anyway. Inside the deep night,
as the house sailed west, he woke up
to hear voices murmuring. And froze.
Then understood it was only the radio.
He got up and went downstairs. He had
to pee anyway. A little rain
that hadn't been there before was
falling outside. The voices
on the radio faded and then came back
as if from a long way. It wasn't
the same station any longer. A man's voice
said something about Borodin,
and his opera *Prince Igor*. The woman
he said this to agreed, and laughed.
Began to tell a little of the story.
The man's hand drew back from the switch.
Once more he found himself in the presence
of mystery. Rain. Laughter. History.
Art. The hegemony of death.
He stood there, listening.

IN SWITZERLAND

First thing to do in Zurich
is take the No. 5 "Zoo" trolley
to the end of the track,
and get off. Been warned about
the lions. How their roars
carry over from the zoo compound
to the Flutern Cemetery.
Where I walk along
the very beautiful path
to James Joyce's grave.
Always the family man, he's here
with his wife, Nora, of course.
And his son, Giorgio,
who died a few years ago.
Lucia, his daughter, his sorrow,
still alive, still confined
in an institution for the insane.
When she was brought the news
of her father's death, she said:
What is he doing under the ground, that idiot?
When will he decide to come out?
He's watching us all the time.
I lingered a while. I think
I said something aloud to Mr. Joyce.
I must have. I know I must have.
But I don't recall what,
now, and I'll have to leave it at that.

A week later to the day, we depart
Zurich by train for Lucerne.
But early that morning I take
the No. 5 trolley once more

to the end of the line.
The roar of the lions falls over
the cemetery, as before.
The grass has been cut.
I sit on it for a while and smoke.
Just feels good to be there,
close to the grave. I didn't
have to say anything this time.

That night we gambled at the tables
at the Grand Hotel-Casino
on the very shore of Lake Lucerne.
Took in a strip show later.
But what to do with the memory
of that grave that came to me
in the midst of the show,
under the muted, pink stage light?
Nothing to do about it.
Or about the desire that came later,
crowding everything else out,
like a wave.
Still later, we sit on a bench
under some linden trees, under stars.
Made love with each other.
Reaching into each other's clothes for it.
The lake a few steps away.
Afterwards, dipped our hands
into the cold water.
Then walked back to our hotel,
happy and tired, ready to sleep
for eight hours.

All of us, all of us, all of us
trying to save
our immortal souls, some ways

seemingly more round-
about and mysterious
than others. We're having
a good time here. But hope
all will be revealed soon.

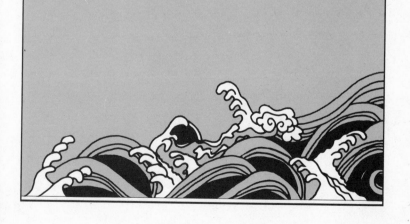

FIVE

A SQUALL

Shortly after three P.M. today a squall
hit the calm waters of the Strait.
A black cloud moving fast,
carrying rain, driven by high winds.

The water rose up and turned white.
Then, in five minutes, was as before—
blue and most remarkable, with just
a little chop. It occurs to me
it was this kind of squall
that came upon Shelley and his friend,
Williams, in the Gulf of Spezia, on
an otherwise fine day. There they were,
running ahead of a smart breeze,
wind-jamming, crying out to each other,
I want to think, in sheer exuberance.
In Shelley's jacket pockets, Keats's poems,
and a volume of Sophocles!
Then something like smoke on the water.
A black cloud moving fast,
carrying rain, driven by high winds.

Black cloud
hastening along the end
of the first romantic period
in English poetry.

MY CROW

A crow flew into the tree outside my window.
It was not Ted Hughes's crow, or Galway's crow.
Or Frost's, Pasternak's, or Lorca's crow.
Or one of Homer's crows, stuffed with gore,
after the battle. This was just a crow.
That never fit in anywhere in its life,
or did anything worth mentioning.
It sat there on the branch for a few minutes.
Then picked up and flew beautifully
out of my life.

THE PARTY

Last night, alone, 3000 miles away from the one
I love, I turned the radio on to some jazz
and made a huge bowl of popcorn
with lots of salt on it. Poured butter over it.
Turned out the lights and sat in a chair
in front of the window with the popcorn and
a can of Coke. Forgot everything important
in the world while I ate popcorn and looked out
at a heavy sea, and the lights of town.
The popcorn runny with butter, covered with
salt. I ate it up until there was nothing
left except a few Old Maids. Then
washed my hands. Smoked a couple more cigarettes
while I listened to the beat of the little
music that was left. Things had quieted way down,
though the sea was still running. Wind gave
the house a last shake when I rose
and took three steps, turned, took three more steps, turned.
Then I went to bed and slept wonderfully,
as always. My God, what a life!
But I thought I should explain, leave a note anyhow,
about this mess in the living room
and what went on here last night. Just in case
my lights went out, and I keeled over.
Yes, there was a party here last night.
And the radio's still on. Okay.
But if I die today, I die happy—thinking
of my sweetheart, and of that last popcorn.

AFTER RAINY DAYS

After rainy days and the same serious doubts—
strange to walk past the golf course,
sun overhead, men putting, or teeing, whatever
they do on those green links. To the river that flows
past the clubhouse. Expensive houses on either side
of the river, a dog barking at this kid
who revs his motorcycle. To see a man fighting
a large salmon in the water just below
the footbridge. Where a couple of joggers have stopped
to watch. Never in my life have I seen anything
like this! Stay with him, I think, breaking
into a run. For Christ's sake, man, hold on!

INTERVIEW

Talking about myself all day
brought back
something I thought over and
done with. What I'd felt
for Maryann—Anna, she calls
herself now—all those years.

I went to draw a glass of water.
Stood at the window for a time.
When I came back
we passed easily to the next thing.
Went on with my life. But
that memory entering like a spike.

BLOOD

We were five at the craps table
not counting the croupier
and his assistant. The man
next to me had the dice
cupped in his hand.
He blew on his fingers, said
Come *on*, baby! And leaned
over the table to throw.
At that moment, bright blood rushed
from his nose, spattering
the green felt cloth. He dropped
the dice. Stepped back amazed.
And then terrified as blood
ran down his shirt. God,
what's happening to me?
he cried. Took hold of my arm.
I heard Death's engines turning.
But I was young at the time,
and drunk, and wanted to play.
I didn't have to listen.
So I walked away. Didn't turn back, ever,
or find this in my head, until today.

TOMORROW

Cigarette smoke hanging on
in the living room. The ship's lights
out on the water, dimming. The stars
burning holes in the sky. Becoming ash, yes.
But it's all right, they're supposed to do that.
Those lights we call stars.
Burn for a time and then die.
Me hell-bent. Wishing
it were tomorrow already.
I remember my mother, God love her,
saying, Don't wish for tomorrow.
You're wishing your life away.
Nevertheless, I wish
for tomorrow. In all its finery.
I want sleep to come and go, smoothly.
Like passing out of the door of one car
into another. And then to wake up!
Find tomorrow in my bedroom.
I'm more tired now than I can say.
My bowl is empty. But it's my bowl, you see,
and I love it.

GRIEF

Woke up early this morning and from my bed
looked far across the Strait to see
a small boat moving through the choppy water,
a single running light on. Remembered
my friend who used to shout
his dead wife's name from hilltops
around Perugia. Who set a plate
for her at his simple table long after
she was gone. And opened the windows
so she could have fresh air. Such display
I found embarrassing. So did his other
friends. I couldn't see it.
Not until this morning.

HARLEY'S SWANS

I'm trying again. A man has to begin
over and over—to try to think and feel
only in a very limited field, the house
on the street, the man at the corner drug store.
—Sherwood Anderson, from a letter

Anderson, I thought of you when I loitered
in front of the drug store this afternoon.
Held onto my hat in the wind and looked down
the street for my boyhood. Remembered my dad
taking me to get haircuts—

that rack of antlers mounted on a wall
next to the calendar picture of a rainbow
trout leaping clear of the water
with a hook in its jaw. My mother.
How she went with me to pick out
school clothes. That part embarrassing
because I needed to shop in men's wear
for man-sized pants and shirts.
Nobody, then, who could love me,
the fattest kid on the block, except my parents.

So I quit looking and went inside.
Had a Coke at the soda fountain
where I gave some thought to betrayal.
How that part always came easy.
It was what came after that was hard.
I didn't think about you anymore, Anderson.
You'd come and gone in an instant.
But I remembered, there at the fountain,
Harley's swans. How they got there
I don't know. But one morning he was taking

his school bus along a country road
when he came across 21 of them just down
from Canada. Out on this pond
in a farmer's field. He brought his school bus
to a stop, and then he and his grade-schoolers
just looked at them for a while and felt good.

I finished the Coke and drove home.
It was almost dark now. The house
quiet and empty. The way
I always thought I wanted it to be.
The wind blew hard all day.
Blew everything away, or nearly.
But still this feeling of shame and loss.
Even though the wind ought to lay now
and the moon come out soon, if this is
anything like the other nights.
I'm here in the house. And I want to try again.
You, of all people, Anderson, can understand.

SIX

ELK CAMP

Everyone else sleeping when I step
to the door of our tent. Overhead,
stars brighter than stars ever were
in my life. And farther away.
The November moon driving
a few dark clouds over the valley.
The Olympic Range beyond.

I believed I could smell the snow that was coming.
Our horses feeding inside
the little rope corral we'd thrown up.
From the side of the hill the sound
of spring water. Our spring water.
Wind passing in the tops of the fir trees.
I'd never smelled a forest before that
night, either. Remembered reading how
Henry Hudson and his sailors smelled
the forests of the New World
from miles out at sea. And then the next thought—
I could gladly live the rest of my life
and never pick up another book.
I looked at my hands in the moonlight
and understood there wasn't a man,
woman, or child I could lift a finger
for that night. I turned back and lay
down then in my sleeping bag.
But my eyes wouldn't close.

The next day I found cougar scat
and elk droppings. But though I rode
a horse all over that country,
up and down hills, through clouds

and along old logging roads,
I never saw an elk. Which was
fine by me. Still, I was ready.
Lost to everyone, a rifle strapped
to my shoulder. I think maybe
I could have killed one.
Would have shot at one, anyway.
Aimed just where I'd been told—
behind the shoulder at the heart
and lungs. "They might run,
but they won't run far.
Look at it this way," my friend said.
"How far would you run with a piece
of lead in your heart?" That depends,
my friend. That depends. But that day
I could have pulled the trigger
on anything. Or not.
Nothing mattered anymore
except getting back to camp
before dark. Wonderful
to live this way! Where nothing
mattered more than anything else.
I saw myself through and through.
And I understood something, too,
as my life flew back to me there in the woods.

And then we packed out. Where the first
thing I did was take a hot bath.
And then reach for this book.
Grow cold and unrelenting once more.
Heartless. Every nerve alert.
Ready to kill, or not.

THE WINDOWS OF THE
SUMMER VACATION HOUSES

They withheld judgment, looking down at us
silently, in the rain, in our little boat—
as three lines went into the dark water
for salmon. I'm talking of the Hood Canal
in March, when the rain won't let up.
Which was fine by me. I was happy
to be on the water, trying out
new gear. I heard of the death,
by drowning, of a man I didn't know.
And the death in the woods of another,
hit by a snag. *They don't call them*
widow-makers for nothing.
Hunting stories of bear,
elk, deer, cougar—taken in and out
of season. More hunting stories.
Women, this time. And this time
I could join in. It used to be girls.
Girls of 15, 16, 17, 18—and we
the same age. Now it was women. And married
women at that. No longer girls. Women.
Somebody or other's wife. The mayor
of this town, for instance. His wife.
Taken. The deputy sheriff's wife, the same.
But he's an asshole, anyway.
Even a brother's wife. *It's not anything*
to be proud of, but somebody had to go
and do his homework for him. We caught
two small ones, and talked a lot, and laughed.
But as we turned in to the landing

a light went on in one of those houses
where nobody was supposed to be.
Smoke drifted up from the chimney
of this place we'd looked at as empty.
And suddenly, like that—I remembered Maryann.
When we were both young.
The rare coin of those mint days!
It was there and gone
by the time we hooked the boat to the trailer.
But it was something to recall.
It turned dark as I watched the figure
move to stand at the window and look

down. And I knew then those things that happened
so long ago must have happened, but not
to us. No, I don't think people could go on living
if they had lived those things. It couldn't
have been us.

The people I'm talking about—I'm sure
I must have read about somewhere.
They were not the main characters, no,
as I'd thought at first and for a long
while after. But some others you
sympathized with, even loved, and cried for—
just before they were taken away
to be hanged, or put somewhere.

We drove off without looking back
at the houses. Last night
I cleaned fish in the kitchen.

This morning it was still dark
when I made coffee. And found blood
on the porcelain sides of the sink.

More blood on the counter. A trail
of it. Drops of blood on the bottom
of the refrigerator where the fish
lay wrapped and gutted.
Everywhere this blood. Mingling with thoughts
in my mind of the time we'd had—
that dear young wife, and I.

MEMORY

Cutting the stems from a quart
basket of strawberries—the first
this spring—looking forward to how
I would eat them tonight, when I was
alone, for a treat (Tess being away),
I remembered I forgot to pass along
a message to her when we talked:
somebody whose name I forget
called to say Susan Powell's
grandmother had died, suddenly.
Went on working with the strawberries.
But remembered, too, driving back
from the store. A little girl
on roller skates being pulled along
the road by this big friendly-
looking dog. I waved to her.
She waved back. And called out
sharply to her dog, who kept
trying to nose around
in the sweet ditch grass.
    It's nearly dark outside now.
Strawberries are chilling.
A little later on, when I eat them,
I'll be reminded again—in no particular
order—of Tess, the little girl, a dog,
roller skates, memory, death, etc.

AWAY

I had forgotten about the quail that live
on the hillside over behind Art and Marilyn's
place. I opened up the house, made a fire,
and afterwards slept like a dead man.
The next morning there were quail in the drive
and in the bushes outside the front window.
I talked to you on the phone.
Tried to joke. Don't worry
about me, I said, I have the quail
for company. Well, they took flight
when I opened the door. A week later
and they still haven't come back. When I look
at the silent telephone I think of quail.
When I think of the quail and how they
went away, I remember talking to you that morning
and how the receiver lay in my hand. My heart—
the blurred things it was doing at the time.

MUSIC

Franz Liszt eloped with Countess Marie d'Agoult,
who wrote novels. Polite society washed its hands
of him, and his novelist-countess-whore.
Liszt gave her three children, and music.
Then went off with Princess Wittgenstein.
Cosima, Liszt's daughter, married
the conductor, Hans von Bülow.
But Richard Wagner stole her. Took her away
to Bayreuth. Where Liszt showed up one morning.
Long white hair flouncing.
Shaking his fist. Music. Music!
Everybody grew more famous.

PLUS

"Lately I've been eating a lot of pork.
Plus, I eat too many eggs and things,"
this guy said to me in the doc's office.
"I pour on the salt. I drink twenty cups
of coffee every day. I smoke.
I'm having trouble with my breathing."
Then lowered his eyes.
"Plus, I don't always clear off the table
when I'm through eating. I forget.
I just get up and walk away.
Goodbye until the next time, brother.
Mister, what do you think's happening to me?"
He was describing my own symptoms to a T.
I said, "What do you think's happening?
You're losing your marbles. And then
you're going to die. Or vice versa.
What about sweets? Are you partial
to cinnamon rolls and ice cream?"
"Plus, I crave all that," he said.
By this time we were at a place called Friendly's.
We looked at menus and went on talking.
Dinner music played from a radio
in the kitchen. It was our song, see.
It was our table.

ALL HER LIFE

I lay down for a nap. But every time I closed my eyes,
mares' tails passed slowly over the Strait
toward Canada. And the waves. They rolled up on the beach
and then back again. You know I don't dream.
But last night I dreamt we were watching
a burial at sea. At first I was astonished.
And then filled with regret. But you
touched my arm and said, "No, it's all right.
She was very old, and he'd loved her all her life."

THE HAT

Walking around on our first day
in Mexico City, we come to a sidewalk café
on Reforma Avenue where a man in a hat
sits drinking a beer.
At first the man seems just like any
other man, wearing a hat, drinking a beer
in the middle of the day. But next to this man,
asleep on the broad sidewalk, is a bear
with its head on its paws. The bear's
eyes are closed, but not all the way. As if
it were there, and not there. Everyone

is giving the bear a wide berth.
But a crowd is gathering, too, bulging
out onto the Avenue. The man has
a chain around his waist. The chain
goes from his lap to the bear's collar,
a band of steel. On the table
in front of the man rests an iron bar
with a leather handle. And as if this
were not enough, the man drains the last
of his beer and picks up his bar.
Gets up from the table and hauls
on the chain. The bear stirs, opens its
mouth—old brown and yellow fangs.
But fangs. The man jerks on the chain,
hard. The bear rises to all fours now
and growls. The man slaps the bear on
its shoulder with the bar, bringing
a tiny cloud of dust. Growls something
himself. The bear waits while the man takes
another swing. Slowly, the bear rises

onto its hind legs, swings at air and at
that goddamned bar. Begins to shuffle
then, begins to snap its jaws as the man
slugs it again, and, yes, again

with that bar. There's a tamborine.
I nearly forgot that. The man shakes
it as he chants, as he strikes the bear
who weaves on its hind legs. Growls
and snaps and weaves in a poor dance.
This scene lasts forever. Whole seasons
come and go before it's over and the bear
drops to all fours. Sits down on its
haunches, gives a low, sad growl.
The man puts the tamborine on the table.
Puts the iron bar on the table, too.
Then he takes off his hat. No one
applauds. A few people see
what's coming and walk away. But not
before the hat appears at the edge
of the crowd and begins to make its
way from hand to hand
through the throng. The hat
comes to me and stops. I'm holding
the hat, and I can't believe it.
Everybody staring at it.
I stare right along with them.
You say my name, and in the same breath
hiss, "For God's sake, pass it along."
I toss in the money I have. Then
we leave and go on to the next thing.

Hours later, in bed, I touch you
and wait, and then touch you again.
Whereupon, you uncurl your fingers.

I put my hands all over you then—
your limbs, your long hair even, hair
that I touch and cover my face with,
and draw salt from. But later,
when I close my eyes, the hat
appears. Then the tamborine. The chain.

LATE NIGHT WITH
FOG AND HORSES

They were in the living room. Saying their
goodbyes. Loss ringing in their ears.
They'd been through a lot together, but now
they couldn't go another step. Besides, for him
there was someone else. Tears were falling
when a horse stepped out of the fog
into the front yard. Then another, and
another. She went outside and said,
"Where did you come from, you sweet horses?"
and moved in amongst them, weeping,
touching their flanks. The horses began
to graze in the front yard.
He made two calls: one call went straight
to the sheriff—"someone's horses are out."
But there was that other call, too.
Then he joined his wife in the front
yard, where they talked and murmured
to the horses together. (Whatever was
happening now was happening in another time.)
Horses cropped the grass in the yard
that night. A red emergency light
flashed as a sedan crept in out of fog.
Voices carried out of the fog.
At the end of that long night,
when they finally put their arms around
each other, their embrace was full of
passion and memory. Each recalled
the other's youth. Now something had ended,
something else rushing in to take its place.
Came the moment of leave-taking itself.
"Goodbye, go on," she said.

And the pulling away.
Much later,
he remembered making a disastrous phone call.
One that had hung on and hung on,
a malediction. It's boiled down
to that. The rest of his life.
Malediction.

VENICE

The gondolier handed you a rose.
Took us up one canal
and then another. We glided
past Casanova's palace, the palace of
the Rossi family, palaces belonging
to the Baglioni, the Pisani, and Sangallo.
Flooded. Stinking. What's left
left to rats. Blackness.
The silence total, or nearly.
The man's breath coming and going
behind my ear. The drip of the oar.
We gliding silently on, and on.
Who would blame me if I fall
to thinking about death?
A shutter opened above our heads.
A little light showed through
before the shutter was closed once
more. There is that, and the rose
in your hand. And history.

THE EVE OF BATTLE

There are five of us in the tent, not counting
the batman cleaning my rifle. There's
a lively argument going on amongst my brother
officers. In the cookpot, salt pork turns
alongside some macaroni. But these fine fellows
aren't hungry—and it's a good thing!
All they want is to harrumph about the likes
of Huss and Hegel, anything to pass the time.
Who cares? Tomorrow we fight. Tonight they want
to sit around and chatter about nothing, about
philosophy. Maybe the cookpot isn't there
for them? Nor the stove, or those folding
stools they're sitting on. Maybe there isn't
a battle waiting for them tomorrow morning?
We'd all like that best. Maybe
I'm not there for them, either. Ready
to dish up something to eat. *Un est autre*,
as someone said. I, or another, may as well be
in China. Time to eat, brothers,
I say, handing round the plates. But someone
has just ridden up and dismounted. My batman
moves to the door of the tent, then drops his plate
and steps back. Death walks in without saying
anything, dressed in coat-and-tails.
At first I think he must be looking for the Emperor,
who's old and ailing anyway. That would explain
it. Death's lost his way. What else could it be?
He has a slip of paper in his hand, looks us over
quickly, consults some names.
He raises his eyes. I turn to the stove.
When I turn back, everyone has gone. Everyone

except Death. He's still there, unmoving.
I give him his plate. He's come a long
way. He is hungry, I think, and will eat anything.

EXTIRPATION

A little quietly outstanding uptown
piano music played in the background
as we sat at the bar in the lounge.

Discussing the fate of the last caribou herd in the U.S.
Thirty animals who roam a small corner
of the Idaho Panhandle. Thirty animals

just north of Bonner's Ferry,
this guy said. Then called for another round.
But I had to go. We never saw each other again.

Never spoke another word to each other,
or did anything worth getting excited about
the rest of our lives.

THE CATCH

Happy to have these fish!
In spite of the rain, they came
to the surface and took
the No. 14 Black Mosquito.
He had to concentrate,
close everything else out
for a change. His old life,
which he carried around
like a pack. And the new one,
that one too. Time and again
he made what he felt were the most
intimate of human movements.
Strained his heart to see
the difference between a raindrop
and a brook trout. Later,
walking across the wet field
to the car. Watching
the wind change the aspen trees.
He abandoned everyone
he once loved.

MY DEATH

If I'm lucky, I'll be wired every whichway
in a hospital bed. Tubes running into
my nose. But try not to be scared of me, friends!
I'm telling you right now that this is okay.
It's little enough to ask for at the end.
Someone, I hope, will have phoned everyone
to say, "Come quick, he's failing!"
And they will come. And there will be time for me
to bid goodbye to each of my loved ones.
If I'm lucky, they'll step forward
and I'll be able to see them one last time
and take that memory with me.
Sure, they might lay eyes on me and want to run away
and howl. But instead, since they love me,
they'll lift my hand and say "Courage"
or "It's going to be all right."
And they're right. It is all right.
It's just fine. If you only knew how happy you've made me!
I just hope my luck holds, and I can make
some sign of recognition.
Open and close my eyes as if to say,
"Yes, I hear you. I understand you."
I may even manage something like this:
"I love you too. Be happy."
I hope so! But I don't want to ask for too much.
If I'm unlucky, as I deserve, well, I'll just
drop over, like that, without any chance
for farewell, or to press anyone's hand.
Or say how much I cared for you and enjoyed
your company all these years. In any case,
try not to mourn for me too much. I want you to know
I was happy when I was here.

And remember I told you this a while ago—April 1984.
But be glad for me if I can die in the presence
of friends and family. If this happens, believe me,
I came out ahead. I didn't lose this one.

TO BEGIN WITH

He took a room in a port city with a fellow
called Sulieman A. Sulieman and his wife,
an American known only as Bonnie. One thing
he remembered about his stay there
was how every evening Sulieman rapped
at his own front door before entering.
Saying, "Right, hello. Sulieman here."
After that, Sulieman taking off his shoes.
Putting pita bread and humus into his mouth
in the company of his silent wife.
Sometimes there was a piece of chicken
followed by cucumbers and tomatoes.
Then they all watched what passed for TV
in that country. Bonnie sitting in a chair
to herself, raving against the Jews.
At eleven o'clock she would say, "We have to sleep now."

But once they left their bedroom door open.
And he saw Sulieman make his bed on the floor
beside the big bed where Bonnie lay
and looked down at her husband.
They said something to each other in a foreign language.
Sulieman arranged his shoes by his head.
Bonnie turned off the light, and they slept.
But the man in the room at the back of the house
couldn't sleep at all. It was as if
he didn't believe in sleep any longer.
Sleep had been all right, once, in its time.
But it was different now.

Lying there at night, eyes open, arms at his sides,
his thoughts went out to his wife,

and his children, and everything that bore
on that leave-taking. Even the shoes
he'd been wearing when he left his house
and walked out. They were the real betrayers,
he decided. They'd brought him all this way
without once trying to do anything to stop him.
Finally, his thoughts came back to this room
and this house. Where they belonged.
Where he knew he was home.
Where a man slept on the floor of his own bedroom.
A man who knocked at the door of his own house,
announcing his meager arrival. Sulieman.
Who entered his house only after knocking
and then to eat pita bread and tomatoes
with his bitter wife. But in the course of those long nights
he began to envy Sulieman a little.
Not much, but a little. And so what if he did!
Sulieman sleeping on his bedroom floor.
But Sulieman sleeping in the same room,
at least, as his wife.

Maybe it was all right if she snored
and had blind prejudices. She wasn't so bad-
looking, that much was true, and if
Sulieman woke up he could at least
hear her from his place. Know she was there.
There might even be nights when he could reach
over and touch her through the blanket
without waking her. Bonnie. His wife.

Maybe in this life it was necessary to learn
to pretend to be a dog and sleep on the floor
in order to get along. Sometimes
this might be necessary. Who knows
anything these days?

At least it was a new idea and something,
he thought, he might have to try and understand.
Outside, the moon reached over the water
and disappeared finally. Footsteps

moved slowly down the street and came to a stop
outside his window. The streetlight
went out, and the steps passed on.
The house became still and, in one way at least,
like all the other houses—totally dark.
He held onto his blanket and stared at the ceiling.
He had to start over. To begin with—
the oily smell of the sea, the rotting tomatoes.

THE CRANES

Cranes lifting up out of the marshland . . .
My brother brings his fingers to his temples
and then drops his hands.

Like that, he was dead.
The satin lining of autumn.
O my brother! I miss you now, and I'd like to have you back.

Hug you like a grown man
who knows the worth of things.
The mist of events drifts away.

Not in this life, I told you once.
I was given a different set of marching orders.
I planned to go mule-backing across the Isthmus.

Begone, though, if this is your idea of things!
But I'll think of you out there
when I look at those stars we saw as children.

The cranes wallop their wings.
In a moment, they'll find true north.
Then turn in the opposite direction.

SEVEN

A HAIRCUT

So many impossible things have already
happened in this life. He doesn't think
twice when she tells him to get ready:
He's about to get a haircut.

He sits in the chair in the upstairs room,
the room they sometimes joke and refer to
as the library. There's a window there
that gives light. Snow's coming
down outside as newspapers go down
around his feet. She drapes a big
towel over his shoulders. Then
gets out her scissors, comb, and brush.

This is the first time they've been
alone together in a while—with nobody
going anywhere, or needing to do
anything. Not counting the going
to bed with each other. That intimacy.
Or breakfasting together. Another
intimacy. They both grow quiet
and thoughtful as she cuts his hair,
and combs it, and cuts some more.
The snow keeps falling outside.
Soon, light begins to pull away from
the window. He stares down, lost and
musing, trying to read
something from the paper. She says,
"Raise your head." And he does.
And then she says, "See what you think
of it." He goes to look
in the mirror, and it's fine.

It's just the way he likes it,
and he tells her so.

It's later, when he turns on the
porchlight, and shakes out the towel
and sees the curls and swaths of
white and dark hair fly out onto
the snow and stay there,
that he understands something: He's
grownup now, a real, grownup,
middle-aged man. When he was a boy,
going with his dad to the barbershop,
or even later, a teenager, how
could he have imagined his life
would someday allow him the privilege of
a beautiful woman to travel with,
and sleep with, and take his breakfast with?
Not only that—a woman who would
quietly cut his hair in the afternoon
in a dark city that lay under snow
3000 miles away from where he'd started.
A woman who could look at him
across the table and say,
"It's time to put you in the barber's
chair. It's time somebody gave you
a haircut."

HAPPINESS IN CORNWALL

His wife died, and he grew old
between the graveyard and his
front door. Walked with a gait.
Shoulders bent. He let his clothes
go, and his long hair turned white.
His children found him somebody.
A big middle-aged woman with
heavy shoes who knew how to
mop, wax, dust, shop, and carry in
firewood. Who could live
in a room at the back of the house.
Prepare meals. And slowly,
slowly bring the old man around
to listening to her read poetry
in the evenings in front of
the fire. Tennyson, Browning,
Shakespeare, Drinkwater. Men
whose names take up space
on the page. She was the butler,
cook, housekeeper. And after
a time, oh, no one knows or cares
when, they began to dress up
on Sundays and stroll through town.
She with her arm through his.
Smiling. He proud and happy
and with his hand on hers.
No one denied them
or tried to diminish this
in any way. Happiness is
a rare thing! Evenings he

listened to poetry, poetry, poetry
in front of the fire.
Couldn't get enough of that life.

AFGHANISTAN

The sad music of roads lined with larches.
The forest in the distance resting under snow.

The Khyber Pass. Alexander the Great.
History, and lapis lazuli.

No books, no pictures, no knick-knacks please me.
But she pleases me. And lapis lazuli.

That blue stone she wears on her dear finger.
That pleases me exceedingly.

The bucket clatters into the well.
And brings up water with a sweet taste to it.

The towpath along the river. The footpath
Through the grove of almonds. My love

Goes everywhere in her sandals.
And wears lapis lazuli on her finger.

IN A MARINE LIGHT NEAR SEQUIM, WASHINGTON

The green fields were beginning. And the tall, white
farmhouses after the tidal flats and those little sand crabs
that were ready to run, or else turn and square off, if
we moved the rock they lived under. The languor
of that subdued afternoon. The beauty of driving
that country road. Talking of Paris, our Paris.
And then you finding that place in the book
and reading to me about Anna Akhmatova's stay there with
    Modigliani.
Them sitting on a bench in the Luxembourg Gardens
under his enormous old black umbrella
reciting Verlaine to each other. Both of them
"as yet untouched by their futures." When
out in the field we saw
a bare-chested young man with his trousers rolled up,
like an ancient oarsman. He looked at us without curiosity.
Stood there and gazed indifferently.
Then turned his back to us and went on with his work.
As we passed like a beautiful black scythe
through that perfect landscape.

EAGLES

It was a sixteen-inch ling cod that the eagle
dropped near our feet
at the top of Bagley Creek canyon,
at the edge of the green woods.
Puncture marks in the sides of the fish
where the bird gripped with its talons!
That and a piece torn out of the fish's back.
Like an old painting recalled,
or an ancient memory coming back,
that eagle flew with the fish from the Strait
of Juan de Fuca up the canyon to where
the woods begin, and we stood watching.
It lost the fish above our heads,
dropped for it, missed it, and soared on
over the valley where wind beats all day.
We watched it keep going until it was
a speck, then gone. I picked up
the fish. That miraculous ling cod.
Came home from the walk and—
why the hell not?—cooked it
lightly in oil and ate it
with boiled potatoes and peas and biscuits.
Over dinner, talking about eagles
and an older, fiercer order of things.

YESTERDAY, SNOW

Yesterday, snow was falling and all was chaos.
I don't dream, but in the night I dreamed
a man offered me some of his whiskey.
I wiped the mouth of the bottle
and raised it to my lips.
It was like one of those dreams of falling
where, they say, if you don't wake up
before you hit the ground,
you'll die. I woke up! Sweating.
Outside, the snow had quit.
But, my God, it looked cold. Fearsome.
The windows were ice to the touch
when I touched them. I got back
in bed and lay there the rest of the night,
afraid I'd sleep again. And find
myself back in that dream . . .
The bottle rising to my lips.
The indifferent man
waiting for me to drink and pass it on again.
A skewed moon hangs on until morning,
and a brilliant sun.
Before now, I never knew what it meant
to "spring out of bed."
      All day snow flopping off roofs.
The crunch of tires and footsteps.
Next door, there's an old fellow shoveling.
Every so often he stops and leans
on his shovel, and rests, letting
his thoughts go where they may.
Staying his heart.
Then he nods and grips his shovel.
Goes on, yes. Goes on.

READING SOMETHING IN
THE RESTAURANT

This morning I remembered the young man
with his book, reading at a table
by the window last night. Reading
amidst the coming and going of dishes
and voices. Now and then he looked
up and passed his finger across
his lips, as if pondering something,
or quieting the thoughts inside
his mind, the going
and coming inside his mind. Then
he lowered his head and went back
to reading. That memory
gets into my head this morning
with the memory of
the girl who entered the restaurant
that time long ago and stood shaking her hair.
Then sat down across from me
without taking her coat off.
I put down whatever book it was
I was reading, and she at once
started to tell me there was
not a snowball's chance in hell
this thing was going to fly.
She knew it. Then I came around
to knowing it. But it was
hard. This morning, my sweet,
you ask me what's new
in the world. But my concentration
is shot. At the table next
to ours a man laughs and laughs
and shakes his head at what

another fellow is telling him.
But what was that young man reading?
Where did that woman go?
I've lost my place. Tell me what it is
you wanted to know.

A POEM NOT AGAINST SONGBIRDS

Lighten up, songbirds. Give me a break.
No need to carry on this way,
even if it is morning. I need more sleep.

Where were you keeping yourselves when I was thirty?
When the house stayed dark and quiet all day,
as if somebody had died?

And this same somebody, or somebody else,
cooked a huge, morose meal for the survivors.
A meal that lasted ten years.

Go on, sweethearts. Come back in an hour,
my friends. Then I'll be wide awake.
You'll see. This time I can promise.

LATE AFTERNOON, APRIL 8, 1984

A little sport-fishing boat
        wallowing
in the rough waters of the Strait.
I put the glasses on him.
Old guy in a canvas hat,
looking grim. Worried,
as he should be.
The other boats have come in
long ago, counting
their blessings.
This fisherman
had to be clear out to Green Point
where giant halibut school.
When the wind struck!
Such force it bent the trees
and caused the water
to stand up.
As it's standing now.

But he'll make it!
If he keeps the bow into
the wind, and if he's lucky.
Even so I look up
the Coast Guard emergency number.
But I don't use it.
I keep watching—an hour, maybe less—
who knows what passes
through his mind, and mine,
in that time?
Then he turns in to the harbor,
where at once it grows calmer.
Takes off his hat then and waves it

like mad—like an old-time cowboy!
Something he won't ever forget.
You betcha.
　　　Me neither.

MY WORK

I look up and see them starting
down the beach. The young man
is wearing a packboard to carry the baby.
This leaves his hands free
so that he can take one of his wife's hands
in his, and swing his other. Anyone can see
how happy they are. And intimate. How steady.
They are happier than anyone else, and they know it.
Are gladdened by it, and humbled.
They walk to the end of the beach
and out of sight. That's it, I think,
and return to this thing governing
my life. But in a few minutes

they come walking back along the beach.
The only thing different
is that they have changed sides.
He is on the other side of her now,
the ocean side. She is on this side.
But they are still holding hands. Even more
in love, if that's possible. And it is.
Having been there for a long time myself.
Theirs has been a modest walk, fifteen minutes
down the beach, fifteen minutes back.
They've had to pick their way
over some rocks and around huge logs,
tossed up from when the sea ran wild.

They walk quietly, slowly, holding hands.
They know the water is out there
but they're so happy that they ignore it.
The love in their young faces. The surround of it.

Maybe it *will* last forever. If they are lucky,
and good, and forebearing. And careful. If they
go on loving each other without stint.
Are true to each other—that most of all.
As they will be, of course, as they will be,
as they know they will be.
I go back to my work. My work goes back to me.
A wind picks up out over the water.

THE TRESTLE

I've wasted my time this morning, and I'm deeply ashamed.
I went to bed last night thinking about my dad.
About that little river we used to fish—Butte Creek—
near Lake Almanor. Water lulled me to sleep.
In my dream, it was all I could do not to get up
and move around. But when I woke early this morning
I went to the telephone instead. Even though
the river was flowing down there in the valley,
in the meadows, moving through ditch clover.
Fir trees stood on both sides of the meadows. And I was there.
A kid sitting on a timber trestle, looking down.
Watching my dad drink from his cupped hands.
Then he said, "This water's so good.
I wish I could give my mother some of this water."
My dad still loved her, though she was dead
and he'd been away from her for a long time.
He had to wait some more years
until he could go where she was. But he loved
this country where he found himself. The West.
For thirty years it had him around the heart,
and then it let him go. He went to sleep one night
in a town in northern California
and didn't wake up. What could be simpler?

I wish my own life, and death, could be so simple.
So that when I woke on a fine morning like this,
after being somewhere I wanted to be all night,
somewhere important, I could move most naturally
and without thinking about it, to my desk.

Say I did that, in the simple way I've described.
From bed to desk back to childhood.

From there it's not so far to the trestle.
And from the trestle I could look down
and see my dad when I needed to see him.
My dad drinking that cold water. My sweet father.
The river, its meadows, and firs, and the trestle.
That. Where I once stood.

I wish I could do that
without having to plead with myself for it.
And feel sick of myself
for getting involved in lesser things.
I know it's time I changed my life.
This life—the one with its complications
and phone calls—is unbecoming,
and a waste of time.
I want to plunge my hands in clear water. The way
he did. Again and then again.

FOR TESS

Out on the Strait the water is whitecapping,
as they say here. It's rough, and I'm glad
I'm not out. Glad I fished all day
on Morse Creek, casting a red Daredevil back
and forth. I didn't catch anything. No bites
even, not one. But it was okay. It was fine!
I carried your dad's pocketknife and was followed
for a while by a dog its owner called Dixie.
At times I felt so happy I had to quit
fishing. Once I lay on the bank with my eyes closed,
listening to the sound the water made,
and to the wind in the tops of the trees. The same wind
that blows out on the Strait, but a different wind, too.
For a while I even let myself imagine I had died—
and that was all right, at least for a couple
of minutes, until it really sank in: *Dead*.
As I was lying there with my eyes closed,
just after I'd imagined what it might be like
if in fact I never got up again, I thought of you.
I opened my eyes then and got right up
and went back to being happy again.
I'm grateful to you, you see. I wanted to tell you.

RAYMOND CARVER is the author of three collections of short stories: *Will You Please Be Quiet, Please?*, which was nominated for the National Book Award; *What We Talk About When We Talk About Love*; and *Cathedral*, which was nominated for the National Book Critics Circle Award and was runner-up for the Pulitzer Prize. He is also the author of *Fires: Essays, Poems, Stories* and of three collections of poetry and numerous chapbooks and limited editions. He was born in 1939 in Clatskanie, Oregon, and currently lives in Port Angeles, Washington, and Syracuse, New York. He was a Guggenheim Fellow in 1979 and has twice been awarded grants by the National Endowment for the Arts. In 1983 he received the prestigious Mildred and Harold Strauss Living Award.